DISCARD

Gray As a Dolphin

written by **Molly Dingles**

illustrated by **Walter Velez**

dingles & company New Jersey

First prebound printing

PUBLISHED BY dingles&company
P.O. Box 508 • Sea Girt, New Jersey • 08750
WEBSITE: www.dingles.com • E-MAIL: info@dingles.com

Library of Congress Catalog Card No.: 2004092985
ISBN: 1-59646-343-0

Printed in the United States of America

●

ART DIRECTED & DESIGNED BY Barbie Lambert
ART ASSISTANT Erin Collity

EDITED BY Andrea Curley

EDUCATION CONSULTANT Kathleen P. Miller
PREPRESS BY Pixel Graphics, Inc.

For Nikkiann

Molly Dingles

is the author of *Jinka Jinka Jelly Bean* and *Little Lee Lee's Birthday Bang*. As Judy Zocchi, she has written the *Paulie & Sasha* series. She is a writer and lyricist who holds a bachelor's degree in fine arts/theater from Mount Saint Mary's College and a master's degree in educational theater from New York University. She lives in Manasquan, New Jersey, with her husband, David.

Walter Velez

was born in New York. He attended the High School of Art and Design and later the School of Visual Arts. He has done illustration work for many major book and gaming companies. He is known for the popular series *Thieves World* as well as the *Myth* series for Ace Books. He has also produced trading cards for *Goosebumps* and *Dune*. In addition, Walter has illustrated several *Star Wars* books for Random House. He lives in Queens, New York, with his wife, Kriti, and daughter, Kassandra.

The Community of Color series is more than just a series of books about colors. The series demonstrates how individual people, places, and things combine to form a community. It allows children to view the world in segments and then experience the wonderment and value of the community as a whole.

Gray as a dolphin

Gray clouds
in the sky

Gray as a whale

Gray pigeons fly.

Gray as a rooftop

Gray bucket for bait

Gray as a shark

Gray exit gate.

Gray as an otter

Gray **family of eels**

Gray as a rat

Gray silly seals.

The color Gray is all around.